RAINTREE
SCIENCE
ADVENTURES

THE RAIN FOREST

Helen H. Carey and Judith E. Greenberg
Illustrated by Bob Masheris

Raintree Publishers
Milwaukee

For Evan — **H.C.**
To Jason, Brian, and Toby — **J.G.**

Editorial

Barbara J. Behm, Project Editor
Judith Smart, Editor-in-Chief

Art/Production

Suzanne Beck, Art Director
Kathleen A. Hartnett, Designer
Andrew Rupniewski, Production Manager
Eileen Rickey, Typesetter

Reviewed for accuracy by:

Gretchen M. Alexander, Executive Director
West 40 Educational Service Center Number 5
Northlake, Illinois

Scott R. Welty, Instructor
Maine East High School
Park Ridge, Illinois

Library of Congress Number: 89-78282

1 2 3 4 5 6 7 8 9   94 93 92 91 90

Library of Congress Cataloging-in-Publication Data
Carey, Helen H.
  The rain forest / by Helen H. Carey and Judith E. Greenberg;
illustrated by Robert Masheris.
  (Raintree science adventures)
  Summary: Describes the plants and animals of the rain forest and discusses the need for preserving the rain forest. 1. Rain-forest fauna—Juvenile literature. 2. Rain-forest plants—Juvenile literature. 3. Rain-forest ecology—Juvenile literature. [1. Rain-forest ecology. 2. Ecology.] I. Greenberg, Judith E. II. Masheris, Robert, ill. III. Title. IV. Series.

QL112.G73 1990 574.5'2642   577.34 — DC21   89-78282
ISBN 0-8172-3753-4 (lib. bdg.)

Before You Begin

This book takes *you* on an adventure in a tropical rain forest! During your adventure, you will fly in a hot-air balloon over the tops of the trees. You will see the beautiful flowers and the monkeys, butterflies, and birds that live in the rain forest.

In the rain forest, you will also take part in an experiment. You will learn how the rain forest is naturally kept healthy and growing.

Knowing the words below will help you in your adventure.

binoculars   a hand-held instrument containing two telescopes that make things far away look bigger

biologist   a scientist who studies plant and animal life

canopy   a rooflike covering. The canopy of a rain forest is made up of the branches and leaves of the tallest trees, which cover and shade the rest of the forest.

clearing   land cleared of trees and brush

entomologist   a scientist who studies insects

extinct   no longer existing

liana   a type of climbing vine

understory   the area in a rain forest that is located between the canopy and the floor

Now turn the page, and begin your science adventure!

Into the Rain Forest

From the air, the rain forest looks like an endless green carpet. The green is broken only by the many small rivers that flow into one big river. You learn that the area of very dense trees and other plants in the rain forest is called the jungle.

The plane circles the small airport on the edge of the jungle. You see a village and a research station below. Your brother, sitting beside you on the plane, is a scientist who studies insects. He is called an **entomologist.** He has asked you to come with him on this trip while he studies rain-forest insects.

The plane lands, and your brother goes to get the suitcases and his scientific equipment. It is hot in the sun. You feel something pull at your shoelace. Something furry is wrapping itself around your ankle!

You look down into the friendly face of a little monkey.

When you reach to pet him, the monkey scampers away, into the jungle. You run after him but stop when a blue butterfly flutters across your path. You can catch up with the butterfly if you hurry.

The bright blue wings of the butterfly sparkle in the sun. When you get near, it flies away again, each time to a taller bush. You get a final look at the butterfly as it darts through the tall trees.

You start to go back to the airport, but it is nowhere in sight. You realize that you don't know which way to turn. Every tree looks the same. You are lost!

As you look around, you think that the best thing to do is to stand still. Your brother will have a better chance of finding you if you don't wander.

You hear voices. The village must be nearby. Suddenly you see the friendly little monkey sitting in a tree in front of you. You decide to follow him back to the **clearing.**

The monkey scampers through the tree branches overhead. You keep up with him on the ground. When you get back to the clearing where the airport is, the monkey runs and jumps onto the head of a boy just about your age. You walk over to the boy.

"We've been looking for you. I'm glad that you are all right," says your brother as he runs toward you. Your brother smiles at the boy with the monkey on his head. "This is Julio Vargas. He lives in the village. Julio is going to help you learn about the rain forest."

Julio smiles at you and snaps his fingers three times. At this sign, the monkey leaps from Julio's head to your shoulder. You and Julio laugh together. You are glad that Julio is going to be your friend.

You and your brother take the suitcases to the house where you are going to stay. You meet Dr. Vargas, Julio's father, there. He also studies insects. He tells you that he can show you where there are ants that grow their own food. You never liked ants before, but Dr. Vargas makes you think they might be exciting.

Your brother turns to you and says, "Before you see the insects and other animals, why don't you look at the trees themselves? There's a platform you can climb. Watch out for the snakes!"

The Floor, the Understory, and the Canopy

In the rain forest, green plants cover the entire land. Small trees sprout from the trunks of tall trees. Ferns are found everywhere. Vines crawl around, over, and under the trees and other plants.

As you stand on the ground, you are on the floor of the rain forest. The tops of the trees that you saw from the airplane make up the **canopy** of the rain forest. The area between the canopy and the floor is called the **understory.** The canopy, the understory, and the floor each have their own particular plants and animals.

The understory of the rain forest is so leafy that at first you do not see the research platform. Julio shows you the steps to climb. Then he swings up on a thick vine.

"Catch!" shouts Julio when you reach the platform. He pushes something that looks like a big snake at you.

You jump back and yell, "That's a boa constrictor! It'll choke me to death!"

Julio laughs and tells you that it's not a snake. It's a type of climbing vine called a **liana.** He also explains that boa constrictors can make good pets.

After you study the rain forest for a while, you and Julio climb down from the platform. Later on, you hang on tight to some lianas and swing like Tarzan. You have great fun!

While you are resting for a moment, you suddenly feel big drops of water landing on your head. Soon the rain comes down so hard that you cannot see Julio standing beside you. You feel as though you are standing under a waterfall. Heavy rains like this happen almost every day in the rain forest. The rain and the warm temperatures make rain-forest trees and other plants grow much bigger than the plants you are used to.

The rain stops as suddenly as it began, and you see some of the animals of the forest. They have come out of the shadows to drink water from the puddles. Some birds drink water from leaves shaped like cups.

You see tree frogs, an iguana, monkeys, storks, a toucan, hummingbirds, and macaws. Flowers are everywhere, too. They attract butterflies and other insects.

"Winter never comes to the rain forest, so flowers grow all the time," says Julio, pointing to a blossom. "Look at that tree trunk. Flowers are growing right on the tree! Some of the most beautiful flowers are found on the tallest trees and vines."

You look at your watch. It's time to get back to the village. Your brother has planned for you to go up in a hot-air balloon to get a better look at the rain-forest canopy.

You race Julio to the clearing, where your brother and the balloon pilot are waiting for you.

Jaguar

Iguana

Fruit bats

Howler monkeys

Four-eyed opossum

Parrot snake

13

You and Julio climb into the basket of the balloon. You give a "thumbs up" sign to the pilot. The blower that is heating the air in the balloon is making so much noise that you can't hear what Julio is saying. He points to a pair of **binoculars**. You look at the rain forest through them.

In the air, the balloon glides slowly above the rain-forest canopy. Playful monkeys swing boldly from branches and vines. Flying squirrels glide from one tree to another. Birds by the hundreds take to the air as your balloon floats by. You see parrots in various brilliant colors. Thousands of butterflies, as big as small birds, dart among the beautiful flowers.

The birds in the canopy like to eat the fruit that grows on many of the trees. The birds and other animals that live in the canopy spend their lives in the treetops. They are hardly ever seen on the rain-forest floor. Everything they need is found in the topmost branches of the rain forest.

15

Dr. Bean's Experiment

The next day, you and Julio go to the research station. You see many posters and signs about living in the rain forest. You spot a sign that says "JUNGLE ROT EXPERIMENT." The scientist working at this table is Dr. Fred Bean. On his worktable are several plastic bags. You wonder what is inside the bags.

"Hi. I'm glad to see you. Do you want to know what I'm doing?" asks Dr. Bean as he points to the bags on the worktable.

You nod yes. You wonder what it could be all about.

"Keeping clothes clean and dry is a big problem for people in the rain forest. However, plants and animals need the rain forest to be wet. These plastic bags will show you how moisture helps living things in the jungle."

Dr. Bean says, "For this experiment, I put a wet, dirty sock in bag number one and placed it in the sun for ten days.

"Bag number two also has a wet, dirty sock. It was put in a closet for ten days.

"A dry, clean sock was put in bag number three, which I placed in the sun for ten days.

"In bag number four, I put another dry, clean sock. It went into the closet for ten days," explains Dr. Bean.

What do you think happened to the socks?

(Write your guess on a piece of paper.)

Dr. Bean is ready to show you the results. He points out that there has been little or no change in the socks in bag numbers one, three, and four. Then he pulls a moldy, dirty sock from bag number two. You pick up the sock and turn your head away because it smells terrible.

"Mildew and mold grew on the dirty, wet sock in the closet," Dr. Bean says. "That's because this particular sock was experiencing conditions similar to those in the rain forest.

"Mildew and mold are both fungi. Fungi are special plants that cannot make their own food. The cotton in the sock was the food for these fungi. Fungi do not need light to grow."

Dr. Bean continues, "In the rain forest, fungi feed on leaves, animal wastes, and other litter on the floor of the rain forest. In this way, fungi keep the rain-forest floor clear. Fungi also help the rain forest grow. For example, when fungi feed on a dead tree branch, they change the wood into substances that make the soil richer. New trees grow in the rich soil. Insects and other animals begin living in the new trees."

You like learning about fungi. Now you want to see the ants that Dr. Vargas has told you grow their own food. Julio says, "Let's go find my father. He's going to work in the rain forest this afternoon."

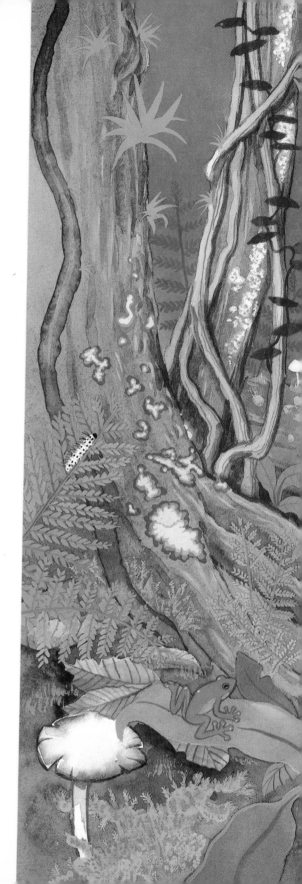

Rain-Forest Ants

You and Julio go into the rain forest with Dr. Vargas.
You stop at a pile of dirt as high as your knees and
several feet around. Dr. Vargas watches the mound
carefully and takes notes. You ask Dr. Vargas what he's
doing. He points to the ground with his pen. You take a
look and see something incredible!

Dime-size pieces of leaves are marching in a long
parade toward the mound. You look more closely.
Under each leaf is a tiny ant! Dr. Vargas explains that
these are leaf-cutting ants. They have scissorlike jaws
that snip pieces out of green leaves. The pieces are
bigger than the ants themselves. The ants carry the
pieces back to the ant nest inside the mound. The nest
goes four or five feet under the ground.

"What happens inside the mound?" you ask.

"The ants use the leaves in their 'food garden' inside the mound," says Dr. Vargas. "The ants chew the leaves until they are mushy and like a paste. They don't eat any of this paste. Instead, they spread it out so fungi can grow on it. The fungi form little round bumps that have liquid inside. This liquid is the ants' food. The ants spend all their lives cutting the leaves, carrying them to the nest, and growing the fungi," explains Dr. Vargas.

"These ants are just like tiny farmers!" you say, shaking your head in amazement.

"Do termites live in the rain forest, too?" you ask.

"Yes. Termites are insects that live wherever there is dead wood. They are important to the rain forest because they eat up fallen trees and other dead wood. Termites are often mistaken for ants, but they are not part of the ant family."

"They sound like tiny garbage disposals," you say.

"That's exactly what they are," says Dr. Vargas. "They do more than get rid of wastes, though. Termites, like fungi, break down dead wood and turn it into useful fertilizer for the soil."

Suddenly, you notice that all the birds around you have flown up into the air. Dr. Vargas immediately grabs you and Julio by your arms. He pulls you away from the leaf-cutter ant mound. "Run!" he shouts. "Run as fast as you can!"

As you run, you wonder what is happening. You hear the noise of thousands of birds flapping and other small animals rustling. Monkeys race through the trees overhead. On the ground, lizards move quickly past you.

Dr. Vargas pushes you and Julio into a nearby concrete hut and slams the metal door. Everyone is out of breath.

"Is a tiger after us?" you ask in a frightened whisper.

"No, not a tiger. Tigers don't live in this rain forest. Look out the window. You'll see what's coming," says Dr. Vargas.

You see an enormous swarm of brownish red ants covering the ground. "Army ants," Dr. Vargas whispers.

Your heart pounds. You watch the ants travel in formation, millions strong. Dr. Vargas explains that these insects are called army ants because some of them are "soldiers" who follow the "scouts." The scouts go ahead of the main army to search for food. The scouts decide which way the army will travel.

Dr. Vargas says, "Army ants eat almost every insect and spider that happens to be in their path. In some cases, they also eat larger animals. They can eat a large frog in minutes, leaving only the clean-picked bones behind." You are glad Julio's friendly little monkey is inside the hut with you.

Just when it looks like the ants are going to swarm over the hut, the army turns away toward the river.

Dr. Vargas lets his breath out in a long sigh. There is no other sound. All the forest creatures in the ants' path have either run away or been eaten. Where the army ants have passed, only skeletons remain.

Exploring the Rain Forest

Early one morning, you and Julio explore the jungle by jeep. Your driver and guide is Dr. Nancy McBurney. She is a **biologist** who likes exploring the rain forest better than working in the laboratory. She is glad you brought your camera and notebook.

"The rain forest is a good place for photography and taking notes. I can help you identify the animals and plants that you see," says Dr. McBurney.

Even early in the morning, the rain forest feels warm and muggy. Your jeep travels slowly along a small river. Dr. McBurney pulls the jeep over to the side of the dirt road so that you can take some pictures of the plants that grow near the river. From the jeep, you look at the water and think that a swim in the river might cool you off.

"Don't even think about swimming here," says Dr. McBurney, guessing your thoughts. "The water contains fish called piranhas. Piranhas are only 12 inches (30 centimeters) long, but they have teeth as sharp as knives." You decide to forget about the swim!

Dr. McBurney points to a mossy log straight ahead near the water. You look more closely at the log. The log has eyes! It's a crocodile! You take a picture of it, but you are very glad to be inside the jeep.

Up ahead, eating water plants, is the strangest animal you have ever seen. It looks as if it weighs hundreds of pounds. It has a body like a pig's, a short trunk something like an elephant's, and a mane like a horse's. Dr. McBurney tells you it is a tapir. You take a picture of it.

"Look over there!" shouts Julio. "There are peccaries!"

You see a group of these wild pigs near a large tree. Peccaries are blackish gray in color and thinner than the pigs you've seen at home. They have pointed hooves.

"Jaguars like to eat tapirs and peccaries," says Dr. McBurney. "However, peccaries can gang up on and trample a jaguar to death. I've even seen a man climb a tree to get away from a peccary."

You see something hanging upside down on a tree branch.

"I think I see a sloth," you say, hoping you are right. "Why doesn't it run away?"

"Yes, that's a sloth," says Dr. McBurney. "A sloth can't run. It moves very slowly. It tries to hide from you by remaining motionless for hours at a time. Sloths can go for a long time without eating or doing anything else."

"Look over there. Isn't that an anteater?" says Julio.

You remember seeing an anteater in the zoo. You get out the binoculars. You watch the anteater rip a hole in an ant's nest. Then it pokes its long, sticky tongue inside to eat the ants.

The jeep comes out of the forest and onto a paved road. You are surprised to see such a modern road right next to the rain forest.

"I want you to see what is happening to the rain forest here and all over the world," says Dr. McBurney sadly.

"All the trees in this part of the rain forest have been cut down. It is extremely hot when there are no trees to keep the sun from baking the ground," Dr. McBurney says. "Scientists worry that without the trees of the rain forest that make shade and give off oxygen, many places in the world will get hotter. This warming could make the various climates throughout the world change.

"The rain forest is home to over one million kinds of plants and animals. Many of these will become **extinct** if the destruction of the rain forest continues."

You turn to Dr. McBurney and ask, "Then why are people cutting down the rain forest?"

"People who cut down the rain forest can sell the trees for lumber. They also think they are getting good farmland. The new farms will have good crops the first year or two. After that, there will be nothing but problems. Without the trees, the important topsoil is washed away by the rain. The ground underneath bakes hard in the sun, and the land is useless," explains Dr. McBurney.

30

Tropical rain forests

Today is the day that you must return home. You will miss Julio and his pet monkey. Most of all, you will miss the beautiful and mysterious rain forest. You have learned that the rain forest is a place where special plants, insects, and other animals have lived for millions of years.

You show your notebook to your brother. You tell him that when you grow up, you want be a scientist. You want to come back to the rain forest to study plants. "Maybe I'll find the right plant that will contain something that can cure a terrible disease," you say.

"No plants for me," says Julio. "I want to be a scientist who studies monkeys!" He snaps his fingers three times. Julio's monkey leaps right onto your head and tickles your ear with its tail.

What kind of science adventure would you like to go on next?